STAY MARRIED
FOR LIFE

FIRST IN THE WINNING AT HOME MARRIAGE SERIES

STAY MARRIED FOR LIFE

ONE-MINUTE REFLECTIONS FOR COUPLES

DAN SEABORN AND PETER NEWHOUSE
WITH SUSAN LEWIS

credo
house publishers

This book is dedicated to our wives and best friends,
Jane Marie Seaborn and Shawn Maree Newhouse.
Our desire is to continue to pray with them
and for them so that we can grow together
and set a good example of marriage for our children.

We trust that you will use these devotionals to nurture
your love for each other and to win at home.

In Christ,

Dan and Peter

TABLE OF CONTENTS

STAY MARRIED FOR LIFE

MALACHI 2:16
"'I hate divorce,' says the Lord God of Israel."

If you think weddings are expensive, consider the cost of divorce. Government studies estimate that divorce costs, on average, approximately $30,000. This includes court and administrative fees, attorney fees, and other expenses. What it doesn't include is an estimate of the emotional cost to you and your spouse, any children involved, or members of your extended family.

While divorce may "seem" like the best solution at times, God's disdain for it is meant to protect you from all the ramifications of it that you don't realize are there. He hates it because of all the pain it causes the couple and many other people who are either directly or indirectly involved. Marriage isn't always easy; but with a little time, effort, energy, and focus blended with compassion and forgiveness, you can stay married for life.

MARRIAGE MOMENTS

❖ What have you done to divorce-proof your marriage?
❖ Have you committed to staying married for life?

PRAY TOGETHER

MIRROR, MIRROR ON THE WALL

1 CORINTHIANS 6:19

"Do you not know that your body is a temple of the Holy Spirit, who is in you, whom you have received from God?"

Many people are running to plastic surgeons these days to maintain a youthful appearance. They are injecting liquids, smearing on wrinkle-free creams or more drastically, seeking surgery to nip, tuck, stretch, or remove skin. This is all done in an effort to fight the aging process—and, sometimes, in an effort to preserve the marriage relationship.

Although it is important to take care of yourself with exercise, a proper diet, and good hygiene, your spouse should ultimately love you for who you are on the inside. The Bible says, "You were bought at a price. Therefore honor God with your body" (1 Corinthians 6:20). If you are constantly worrying about how you look or complaining and trying to change your body, is that honoring to God?

There are more important things in life than image. Once you are content on the inside, you will feel more beautiful on the outside.

MARRIAGE MOMENTS

❖ What steps do you need to take to ensure you are taking care of yourself?

❖ How do you honor God with your body?

PRAY TOGETHER

GOING FOR OLYMPIC GOLD

ECCLESIASTES 4:12
"Though one may be overpowered, two can defend themselves.
A cord of three strands is not quickly broken."

In the Olympics, athletes strive to reach the pinnacle of success by capturing the gold medal in their event. They train, with the help of a coach, and focus for years on that one single skill. What if you had that same attitude toward your spouse? What if you embodied the Olympic spirit throughout your marriage?

Christ wants to be your coach. He wants to be invited into your marriage relationship so that you have a greater chance to achieve the pinnacle of success in your marriage. Every marriage relationship will experience struggles and triumphs. Marriage is more like a marathon than a sprint, so commit in your heart and mind to keep training—through the gold-medal days as well as the bronze. Regardless of the type of day, with Christ at the center of your marriage you'll have a better opportunity of maintaining a winning attitude toward your spouse.

MARRIAGE MOMENTS

❖ How do you keep Christ at the center of your marriage?
❖ What can you do to maintain a "gold-medal attitude"?

PRAY TOGETHER

R.E.S.P.E.C.T.

EPHESIANS 5:33

*"However, each one of you also must love his wife as he loves himself,
and the wife must respect her husband."*

The Lord deserves our respect because of who He is to us—our Savior. Your spouse deserves your respect for the same reason because of who they are to you. With God's guidance and direction, you chose that person as your spouse and, even though they aren't always perfect, they are worthy of your respect because of the choice you have made to be together.

How well do you show respect to your spouse? You might reply that you listen to them attentively, clean up after yourself in the bathroom, or lend a hand when they are in need. But how much do you solicit your spouse's opinion when it comes to decisions, both large and small? Do you respect your spouse's opinion as valid, or is it only valid when other people you trust concur with it?

Consulting with your spouse, respecting their opinion, and including them in your decision-making process is another way to show them how much they are loved. It is a respect they deserve as your partner in life.

MARRIAGE MOMENTS

❖ When was the last time you involved your spouse in a decision, whether large or small?

❖ What other ways can you show your spouse they are respected?

PRAY TOGETHER

A Glass Half Full

ROMANS 12:10

"Be devoted to one another in brotherly love. Honor one another above yourselves."

The Lord commands that you love your neighbor as yourself. He didn't give us that command because it was the easiest to fulfill—in fact, quite the opposite is true. What about your spouse—the closest neighbor you have? Have you ever noticed how easy it is to come up with negative things to say about them? Maybe you complain he doesn't help enough around the house, or maybe she doesn't take an interest in the things you like. By nature, we are more prone to be negative than positive, and being this way toward your spouse can be both hurtful and destructive.

That's why it's important to notice something every day that you love about your spouse. Then tell them what that is at some point during the day. Maybe you can share it first thing in the morning before either of you leave, or bring it up at night before you go to bed. Or maybe you should call your spouse in the middle of the afternoon and declare what it is you love about them. The point is that you want to spend more time building each other up than tearing each other down. This is one practice that can help you create a marriage for life.

MARRIAGE MOMENTS

❖ What can you do to stop communicating negative thoughts about your spouse?

❖ Develop a list of things you love about your spouse.

PRAY TOGETHER

A QUESTION WORTH ASKING

ROMANS 12:9
"Love must be sincere. Hate what is evil; cling to what is good."

Christians spend a lot of time throughout their lives seeking to improve themselves in some way or another in order to better reflect the image of Christ to others. That might be accomplished by taking a class, joining a small group at church, or reading a book to help them better understand what Jesus requires. This same goal applies to other pursuits as well: golfers try to reach a lower score each time they are on the course. Runners try to beat their time in each race they run. Employees improve their skills in order to seek the next promotion.

What if we take that same approach with our spouse? Have you asked your spouse lately how you can improve as a husband/wife? Find a quiet moment when you can be alone, take a deep breath, and reflect on what you can do better. It's a question worth asking to help make your marriage the best it can be.

MARRIAGE MOMENTS

❖ How do you think you can improve as a spouse? Ask your spouse.
❖ How did you feel about what your spouse said?

PRAY TOGETHER

TRUST ME

1 CORINTHIANS 4:2
"Now it is required that those who have been given a trust must prove faithful."

Trust is the cornerstone of a relationship with Christ. You either trust Jesus or you don't; there's no middle ground. The same is true of your spouse. A strong marriage relationship is nurtured by your ability to trust one another. Every single day you have opportunities to build trust with your spouse. You can tell them the truth without withholding important details. You can follow through with words and actions to build trust and confidence with them. You can keep all your promises, no matter how small. You can make your life an open book so that they have no reason not to trust you.

It is important to establish a pattern of trustworthiness in your marriage. This doesn't happen overnight but is created by taking small steps every day to ensure that your spouse can trust you.

MARRIAGE MOMENTS

❖ When have you ever given your spouse a reason not to trust you?
❖ What can you change in your life now that will help build a pattern of trust?

PRAY TOGETHER

REMEMBER WHEN

PHILIPPIANS 1:3
"I thank my God every time I remember you."

Remember when you first fell in love with Christ? Most people who realize what God has done for them experience a time when they're on fire with devotion and gratitude to Him! Remember when you first fell in love with your spouse? You probably had a similar kind of fire, a charge of emotion, a thrill that surrounded this new love. Let your mind travel back to the time when you were dating, and remember what you were like in the days when you were trying to win your spouse's heart. If you have kids, share those stories with them.

You called for no reason at all. You talked about them all the time. You couldn't wipe the grin off your face when they were around. You made efforts to be romantic, to be alluring, and to be impressive. You tried hard to make every aspect of the relationship work.

When we neglect to celebrate the good in a relationship, things can quickly get stale. That's why it's important for husbands and wives to remember and revive those early days, to find small ways to keep things exciting and fresh.

MARRIAGE MOMENTS

❖ Tell your spouse the one thing you remember most about your first meeting.
❖ What can you do to freshen up your relationship?

PRAY TOGETHER

PILLOW TALK

SONG OF SOLOMON 7:10
"I belong to my lover, and his desire is for me."

God created sexual activity to be an incredible force toward good within a marriage. It creates a world where only the two exist, a place reserved for husband and wife alone. Connecting you both physically and emotionally, it unites you in body and spirit. In a sense, it's a physical and emotional adhesive that helps to hold you together—the bond is so powerful it even has a way of smoothing out rough areas in your marriage.

Still, sex can be one of the most difficult discussion topics in a marriage by far. Not only is it deeply personal, with the potential to be very complicated and confusing, but the process of discovering sexual satisfaction is also an ever-changing, always-adapting experience in marriage. That's why it's so vital to regularly communicate about and evaluate your sex life.

MARRIAGE MOMENTS

❖ What messages about sex (from your childhood/culture/church, etc.) have you carried into your marriage?
❖ What one simple adjustment could you make together to have a more satisfying sex life?

PRAY TOGETHER

THIRD-PARTY CHAIR

JAMES 1:19

*"Everyone should be quick to listen, slow to speak
and slow to become angry."*

Every marriage relationship is going to have its fair share of arguments. Oftentimes you and your spouse will not see eye to eye. When this happens, it is time to bring a third party into the dispute in the form of an empty chair from the kitchen table.

Take turns explaining things to the chair. Does that sound unusual? The reason for this is that it is ridiculous to get defensive when you are talking to a chair. You are less likely to raise your voice or blow things out of proportion. Manipulation is impossible and so is talking in circles—seriously, it is a piece of furniture!

The best part of this exercise is that it gets rid of accusations. When explaining things to a third party, you can't say "*you*" anymore. In order to accuse, you'd have to go with "He did this" or "She did that," and it doesn't take long for that to sound just plain whiney.

So with the third-party chair, things can quickly boil down to "*I*" and "*we*"—and that shift in pronouns makes all the difference. On those terms, it seems easier to forgive, easier to give in, easier to get along.

MARRIAGE MOMENTS

❖ When you feel an argument is starting to boil, consider what you would say to a chair.

❖ How quickly do you forgive your spouse after an argument has ended?

PRAY TOGETHER

RED LIGHT, GREEN LIGHT

PSALM 121:5
*"The LORD watches over you—the LORD is your shade
at your right hand."*

As humans, we are easily distracted. That's why Satan loves nothing more than to keep us sidetracked from a relationship with Christ. What are you distracted by? For example, have you ever been distracted at a red light? Does your spouse quickly tell you when the light is green if you don't respond to the change quickly enough? It may be irritating, but it certainly isn't wrong. Some people get distracted at a red light because they are fumbling in their purse, looking at their phone or fiddling with the radio. At these times, a quick reminder from your spouse is helpful.

What other things are like that green light? What kinds of things distract you that could be helped by a quick comment from your spouse? Think about these things, and learn to turn what you consider your spouse's other annoying habits into strengths. It may not be the green light issue but something else that, if viewed another way, could simply be seen as helpful and positive rather than negative.

MARRIAGE MOMENTS

❖ What habits does your spouse have that you consider annoying?
❖ How could those habits be turned from annoying to helpful?

PRAY TOGETHER

There's No "I" in "We"

MARK 10:8

"'And the two will become one flesh.'
So they are no longer two, but one."

When you make a decision to follow Christ, He immediately begins to live in your heart. You are no longer separated from God, but live in unity with Him as one. It's the same concept the moment you say "I do." However, there are days when you might forget about unity and conferring with your spouse about something. It happens when, for example, you both end up making plans for one another on the same day, but they aren't the same plans. When this happens, you will probably find yourself at odds with each other.

Don't lose your "we" mentality and develop a "me" attitude toward each other. Marriage, after all, is by definition the making of one life out of two, which is something that requires constant interaction and consistent communication. And this communication needs to be loving, attentive, and careful. When you do have a communication breakdown, be sure you talk together, figure out what went wrong, and develop a plan so that it doesn't turn into a pattern.

MARRIAGE MOMENTS

❖ How do you approach making plans together?
❖ What can you do to ensure you don't double-book your schedules?

PRAY TOGETHER

Running on Empty

EPHESIANS 4:22-23

"You were taught to be made new in the attitude of your minds."

There are times when Christians "run on empty" when it comes to their relationship with Christ. They live on fumes for a while until they dig back into God's Word and get reignited. Marriages can also run on empty. For a while, both husband and wife are feeling comfortable. He's happy, she's happy, everybody's healthy, the bills are getting paid on time, and sparks are flying in the bedroom.

But then, unexpectedly, circumstances can change. The company downsizes. The spark dwindles. Somebody gets sick. Somebody feels hurt. Or the money isn't stretching far enough, the apology is long overdue, the upbringings collide, the feelings subside.

Is that where your marriage is today—running on empty? Perhaps it's time to flip over to a reserve tank—to love when you don't feel like it, to laugh together just to be laughing again, to forgive when it's not deserved, to hold hands, even halfheartedly, because that's better than nothing.

Believe it or not, your reserve tank might have just enough to get you to the next filling station. And that makes a world of difference.

MARRIAGE MOMENTS

❖ What is the current state of your marriage?
❖ What can you do in the future to ensure you don't run out of fuel?

PRAY TOGETHER

PIT STOP

1 THESSALONIANS 5:16–17

"Be joyful always; pray continually."

If you know anything about NASCAR, you know that drivers have to occasionally make pit stops so that their cars can fill up on fuel, remove worn or damaged parts, and get back in the race. These pit stops are executed with precision and finesse, and are perfectly timed so that the driver does not fall behind in the race. It's the same concept for Christians when they attend a retreat or prayer group or spend time alone with God. They get a spiritual pit stop to refuel, refresh, and get moving again.

Now translate that concept to marriage. Are you getting regular maintenance checkups in your marriage? The type of pit stop a marriage needs might include talking and connecting regularly, putting some date nights on the calendar, and getting away together as a couple. It might be sending your spouse a card in the mail to remind them of your love. These are the things that keep a marriage on track. Stop for the fuel you need to keep your marriage going strong.

MARRIAGE MOMENTS

❖ When did you have your last pit stop?
❖ What can you do to maintain your marriage and keep it in good condition?

PRAY TOGETHER

First-Class Marriage

PHILIPPIANS 4:8

"Whatever is true, whatever is noble, whatever is right, whatever is pure, whatever is lovely, whatever is admirable—if anything is excellent or praiseworthy—think about such things."

If you've ever flown on an airplane you know there are different seating sections—first class, business class, and coach. You pay a higher price for first class, and you get wider seats, impeccable service, and extra space in the overhead bins. Business class costs more as well, and gets the buyer a few extra perks. Think about your marriage. Does it have all the amenities of first class, or are you settling for coach?

In a first-class marriage, spouses give each other a little more elbow room. When your spouse presses the call button, it doesn't take long for you to respond to their needs. When their throat is dry, when the temperature has gotten uncomfortable, when they're having a hard time sleeping, when they just need to pop in a good movie for laughs, you are there for them. Business-class efforts are positive, but don't reflect the effort represented in first class.

A first-class marriage costs more—sometimes a lot more. What makes for this difference? First-class spouses put effort and energy into their relationship, and not everybody is willing to pay that price. When push comes to shove, not everyone wants to win at home.

MARRIAGE MOMENTS

❖ What can you do to make your marriage more first class?
❖ Do you pamper, provide extras, and offer more than what is expected in your marriage?

PRAY TOGETHER

Marriage Getaway

EPHESIANS 4:3
"Make every effort to keep the unity of the Spirit through the bond of peace."

There are several stories in the Bible where Jesus talks about getting away alone to pray. Doing so provided important spiritual nourishment for Him to continue to grow in His ministry. It's the same reason you need to get away with your spouse, although you'll find a million and one excuses for not planning this time away.

For starters, there's the time issue. Between projects at work, commitments around town, kids' activities, reunions with family, outings among friends, and the annual neighborhood block party, your calendar is already set to *buzzing* for the next thirty-eight weeks.

Although kids, schedules, and money come and go in a home, it's the marriage relationship that should last.

If you can set aside time for only each other, you'll get the chance to relax and refresh. You'll be able to put your schedules in perspective, to reach agreements in your finances, and to discuss family situations.

MARRIAGE MOMENTS

❖ When was the last time you and your spouse planned a getaway?
❖ What is standing in the way of you building a bond in your marriage?

PRAY TOGETHER

HEALTHY BOUNDARIES

EXODUS 20:14
"You shall not commit adultery."

Just as Christ wants us to have an exclusive relationship with Him, so also He expects the same commitment between spouses. The commandment to not commit adultery is a testament to that desire. In all walks of life you will be exposed to members of the opposite sex. This will occur at work, the grocery store, church activities, or functions involving your kids. It is important that you create healthy boundaries in your relationships with members of the opposite sex.

Be sure to keep your everyday conversations and interactions from crossing any inappropriate lines. If there's an individual or a circumstance that threatens to get between you and your spouse, do everything possible to avoid that individual or circumstance.

Infidelity doesn't happen by chance, and it can be emotional or relational. Typically, a long pattern of line-crossing happens before sexual indiscretion occurs. Be constantly aware of your surroundings and interactions with others so that you do not compromise your commitment to your spouse. Set up your life in a way that promotes faithfulness and steadfastly hold to your commitment to your spouse.

MARRIAGE MOMENTS

❖ What kind of healthy boundaries have you set up in your relationship with members of the opposite sex?
❖ How can you make yourself accountable to your spouse in your areas of weakness?

PRAY TOGETHER

LISTEN UP!

PROVERBS 1:5

*"Let the wise listen and add to their learning,
and let the discerning get guidance."*

We grow in our relationship with Christ by listening to His word. It is in the silence that we hear the most. When you think about your closest friends, is it mutual interests, shared experiences, or a similar sense of humor that draws you close? Those are important, certainly, but what sets your peers apart from your dearest friends is most likely their ability to listen.

The husband and wife who develop listening skills with each other will benefit from a deeper friendship in their marriage—a stronger bond between them.

It's very possible that the most powerful gift we can give to our spouse is the gift of two good ears. Instead of spacing out, butting in, offering easy answers, speeding up the chatter, forgetting key points, dozing off, changing the subject, or keeping one ear tuned elsewhere, we can do our best to hear what our spouse has to say. We can do this by *active listening*.

MARRIAGE MOMENTS

❖ What would your spouse say about your listening skills?
❖ What do you think you can do to improve your listening skills?

MONEY TALKS

1 PETER 5:2

"Be not greedy for money; but eager to serve"

The apostle Paul warns that the love of money is a root of all kinds of evil. He doesn't say money is evil, but you'd think it was because it's one of the biggest reasons married couples argue. Money talks, but it speaks a different language to different men and women. This should come as no surprise, especially if you consider how many financial questions a husband and wife can answer differently.

The terminology we use is the same—*financial security* is what it's called, on both sides of the gender gap. But to him financial security is a verb, something to do—with emphasis on *securing* finances. To her financial security is a noun, something to have—with emphasis on *secure* finances.

In your marriage, pursuing financial security might be as simple as learning to appreciate your spouse's languages. For the most part, a man's sense of financial well-being comes from action, by getting or increasing money and material possessions. By contrast, financial security for a woman is better understood as a reaction—she *reacts* to the status of the finances.

MARRIAGE MOMENTS

❖ Are you doing what you can to make sure your wife feels financially secure in your marriage?
❖ Have you shown satisfaction in your husband's ability to provide?

PRAY TOGETHER

LAUGHTER IS THE BEST MEDICINE

ECCLESIASTES 3:4

"There is a time to weep and a time to laugh."

Have you ever found yourself saying that God must have a sense of humor because of certain circumstances in your life? Well, He must, because He gave one to each of us, and we're reflective of His image. A healthy sense of humor is a great gift in a marriage; the ability to laugh covers a multitude of ills in the marriage relationship. Some medical professionals maintain that laughter reduces stress, relieves pain, lowers blood pressure, and boosts the immune system. It puts people at ease and can lower tension in your relationships.

The two of you probably laughed a lot more while you were dating. At this point, finances, jobs, kids, and other distractions may be creating more frowns than grins, but it doesn't have to be that way. If you can't remember the last time you and your spouse laughed, then you need to create some laughter moments today. Rent a comedy to watch on DVD, tell some jokes or read the comics and share a hearty belly laugh with your mate. Almost everyone's marriage can use more laughter and fun.

MARRIAGE MOMENTS

❖ Can you remember the last time you really had a good laugh together?

❖ What really makes your spouse chuckle?

PRAY TOGETHER

Mixed (Marriage) Messages

1 JOHN 3:18
*"Dear children, let us not love with words or tongue
but with actions and in truth."*

Jesus spoke in parables, and quite often only those who knew Him would understand them. But even those who knew Him would often have difficulty interpreting the word pictures He used in His teachings.

In the same way, when you speak, are you being clear with your spouse? When you communicate, you send four kinds of messages to your listener, and only one of these is verbal. While your voice transmits a message, you also convey a large amount of information through your appearance, your mannerisms, and your physical behavior. These three types of messages are known as nonverbal communication, or *body language*. This means that effective communication in your marriage takes careful attention—to both words and actions.

Here are some things to try if you want to keep body language from getting in the way of what you're really saying. Convey expressions of love, commitment, and support today by avoiding mixed messages in your marriage. Ease your communication patterns away from distractions and toward sincerity. When you do this, you just might find yourself diffusing arguments more quickly and having fewer silly disagreements with your spouse.

On the flip side of this issue, make the most of what you have to say—give it a boost with body language that matches!

MARRIAGE MOMENTS

❖ What kind of messages is your body language communicating?
❖ What can you do to improve your communication?

PRAY TOGETHER

Marrying Up

1 CORINTHIANS 7:7
"I wish that all men were as I am. But each man has his own gift from God; one has this gift, another has that."

Christians don't deserve the salvation they receive. That's the beauty of this gift. Similarly, some people believe they "married up." They subscribe to the idea that their spouse is the better half and they don't deserve them. They have put their spouse on a pedestal and are continually looking up to them. But in reality, both spouses come to the marriage offering their own unique gifts.

Maybe your spouse is better at finances than you are; but maybe you are better at organization. Each of you has something to offer the other in the relationship. Embrace your differences and celebrate each other's strengths. And if you are in a relationship where you think your spouse is the "lower" half, or even the missing half, then adjust your attitude to change that spirit. Think of some of the things they've done for you that have actually helped you and built you up. Stop focusing on what they haven't or can't do for you. Celebrate their gifts!

MARRIAGE MOMENTS

❖ In which way do you think about your spouse?
❖ If it is not in a good way, what can you do to change your thinking?

PRAY TOGETHER

CHANGE ME

MATTHEW 18:3

"And he said: 'I tell you the truth, unless you change and become like little children, you will never enter the kingdom of heaven.'"

Prayers to God often involve some kind of request to change something or someone. Too often in marriages, couples make the same appeal. *Change my marriage*, they'll say to a counselor. *Change my circumstances*, they'll say to a pastor. *Change my dissatisfaction*, they'll say to a lover, a drug, a bottle, a distraction. *Change who you are*, they'll say to their spouse. All those attempts can lead to change in a marriage, but none of them leads to a complete solution. It's only when we pursue God, when we stand and look at the goodness and unchanging nature of the Creator of the universe, that we can understand why.

The passage above defines God as the ultimate yardstick against which we measure ourselves. In the presence of the One who is fully true, noble, right, pure, lovely, and admirable, a person's perspective shifts. Our selfishness, our shallowness, our trite arguments, and our faults seem trivial when we get to know who God is. All the other minor issues and character flaws filter through, bubble to the surface, and pop. Then and only then can we see the solution for a marriage: *Change what you value and understand what God values.*

MARRIAGE MOMENTS

❖ Are you pursuing God in your marriage?
❖ What can you change about yourself that can help your marriage?

PRAY TOGETHER

COMPETE OR COMPLETE

ROMANS 15:5

*"May the God who gives endurance and encouragement give you
a spirit of unity among yourselves as you follow Christ Jesus."*

Jesus preaches unity and yet, even in our marriages, we sometimes tend to *compete* instead of *complete*. Whether you have been married a week or twenty-five years, there are times in marriage when spouses fall into this competition. Perhaps you feel the need to win every argument. Or you are determined to stand your ground and have things your way. If that's you and your spouse, then you need to find a way to move from *compete* to *complete*.

Figure out what you lack in your character or personality and see whether your spouse can help complete that in you. For example, if you are impatient and your spouse isn't, maybe they can support or help you wait things out longer than you might normally do. Let your spouse help you grow in areas where you are not strong. Let them push you beyond your comfort zone and become a more complete individual.

MARRIAGE MOMENTS

❖ Which mode is your marriage in today: completion or competition?

❖ Ask your spouse how you can complete them more today.

PRAY TOGETHER

LEAVE AND CLEAVE

GENESIS 2:24

*"For this reason a man will leave his father and mother
and be united to his wife, and they will become one flesh."*

God knew the importance of not including your parents as part of your marriage relationship. God is the only third entity that should impact your marriage, and He intended that the "leave and cleave" principle be observed in every marriage. *Leave* means that when you get married, you leave home—your mom and dad, siblings, your previous life. Some of you have still not done that even though you are married. You and your spouse are still arguing about the way things were in your family of origin or you are still going first to your parents for advice instead of talking to your spouse. That's not leaving. And leaving is essential to building your marriage relationship.

Cleave means to stick together. Take your hands, fold them together, interlocking your fingers … that's cleaving. Does that represent your marriage today? Or are your hands slapping against one another? If they are, then perhaps you should consider how you can better cleave to your spouse as a step toward learning to grow together.

MARRIAGE MOMENTS

❖ Have you left your home of origin and joined your spouse in marriage?

❖ What can you do to continue to cleave as a couple?

PRAY TOGETHER

ONE GOOD THING

PSALM 147:1

*"How good it is to sing praises to our God, how pleasant
and fitting to praise him!"*

One of the ways Christians are taught to pray is to begin by speaking praises to the Lord. So often it's easier to jump straight to our requests and forget to praise God for who He is. But praising the Lord first reminds us how good and gracious He is to us.

This principle can apply to our relationships as well. How often do you tell your spouse at least one good thing you appreciate about them? If it's less than three times a week, then consider how you can begin to develop a new habit. Pinpoint one good thing you appreciate about your spouse and start praising them for that every day for a week. You will be amazed at how much taller your spouse is standing, how much more they look forward to seeing you. It will open up communication lines that have been disconnected—possibly for a long, long time.

It's easy after you've been married for a long time to take your spouse for granted. Change that by remembering regularly all the good things your spouse brings to your life.

MARRIAGE MOMENTS

❖ When was the last time you told your spouse one good thing about them?

❖ What are some ways your spouse feels affirmed?

PRAY TOGETHER

FOREVER LOVE

PSALM 100:5
"For the LORD is good and his love endures forever;
his faithfulness continues through all generations."

Your relationship with the Lord will never end as long as you continue to seek His face. If you stop, your relationship will suffer. The same is true for your marriage. Sometimes couples will put their marriage on hold when they have children. That kind of thinking can be detrimental for a couple, especially since the children will eventually leave and you'll be alone together again. It is important that throughout the marriage you continue to cultivate a deep relationship with your spouse. Of course you have a special relationship with your kids as well, but the spousal relationship is different, and you need to let your kids know why it is so important that you make it a priority.

Your children need to see a snapshot of a good marital relationship so they will know how to behave in their own marriage relationships when they are adults. Set a worthy example for your children to follow: make sure your family portrait is complete with a mom and dad who love each other. God's design for family puts Him at the head, your spouse next, and then your children.

MARRIAGE MOMENTS

❖ How much time and attention are you giving to your marriage relationship?
❖ What can you do to further enhance the quality of your marriage?

PRAY TOGETHER

TRIPLE AAA FOR RELATIONSHIPS

EPHESIANS 4:32

"Be kind and compassionate to one another, forgiving each other, just as in Christ God forgave you."

You take out insurance on your home and cars for protection in case a costly repair is ever needed. Myra Kirshenbaum is a therapist who suggests using "Triple AAA" for relationship repairs. There is no phone number to call, but there are a few steps you can take when you are stranded and your relationship is in need of help.

The first A is for apology. Tell your spouse you are sorry. Make sure you do it right away. The second A is for affection. Be sure to show your spouse love and kindness through a gentle hug or touch. The third A makes a promise of action. Agree to take whatever steps are necessary to grow your relationship. God commands us to forgive one another and make repairs when needed in order to restore a broken relationship.

MARRIAGE MOMENTS

❖ Is there a current situation in your marriage that requires Triple AAA?
❖ Which step in this process is the most difficult to take?

PRAY TOGETHER

LUTHER ON LOVE

LAMENTATIONS 3:32
*"Though he brings grief, he will show compassion,
so great is his unfailing love."*

Martin Luther once said, "There is no more lovely, friendly, and charming relationship, communion, or company than a good marriage." For those of you who are in a good season of marriage, you are smiling in agreement. For some people whose marriage is not loving, charming, or in communion right now, they are wondering where it all went wrong.

There is hope for every marriage if you are committed to making it work. Many couples who have been married a long time have experienced moments where they wanted to give up. Many have survived some pretty big issues. You can too! Seek the Lord for the help you need to move forward in your marriage relationship, and enjoy what Luther describes as one of the most rewarding earthly relationships.

MARRIAGE MOMENTS

❖ What season is your marriage currently in?
❖ What can you do to change the season of your marriage so that you are in greater communion?

TWENTY-FIVE REASONS

EPHESIANS 5:22

"Wives, submit to your husbands as to the Lord."

Somebody once wrote a list of twenty-five reasons why women like men. One of the reasons included his shoulder where a woman has a perfect place to lay her head and rest. Another reason was the fact that men are unapologetic when they eat a big steak. Women also claim to appreciate a man's bravery when it comes to snakes and spiders. Even though these may sound somewhat cheesy, men do love to hear what women like about them.

The Lord doesn't command His people to praise Him, but it's something we want to do to show our love and reverence for Him. It's a response from our heart that reflects love back to God.

As wives, maybe you don't think you need to say anything because your husbands know how you feel. But the truth is, men like to hear it. So wives, tell your husbands all the reasons you like them, including the trivial ones that might seem silly. You never know what might be of great encouragement to your husband!

MARRIAGE MOMENTS

❖ What are some of the little things you appreciate about your husband?

❖ What will you do to ensure you verbally share these with him?

Digging Marriage

PSALM 57:10

"For great is your love, reaching to the heavens; your faithfulness reaches to the skies."

Author Agatha Christie once said, "An archeologist is the best husband a woman can have, because the older you get, the more interest he shows in you." If you and your spouse have already been together a long time, maybe this is what you've experienced. If you are newlyweds, just remember the best is yet to come. If you've been married awhile and you feel as though the relationship is deteriorating with age, then it's time to dig deep and find out what is going wrong.

A marriage relationship should get better over time because you know more about your spouse and have learned more about their strengths and weaknesses, their likes and dislikes, their hopes and fears. You have history together and you've made a commitment to love one another as God has loved you. No matter how long you've been married, there's always more to discover about your spouse.

MARRIAGE MOMENTS

❖ Is your marriage better today than it was a year ago? Than five years ago?
❖ What would help your marriage to improve?

PRAY TOGETHER

COUNT ON LOVE

1 PETER 4:8

*"Above all, love each other deeply, because love
covers over a multitude of sins."*

Just imagine if the Lord had decided to accept us or not accept
us based on the number of mistakes we had made in life. How
awful would it be if God's love were conditional on how we acted,
if we were concerned that His love for us would change based on
our behavior?

Now apply that concept to your marriage. What if you added
up all the mistakes you have made in your marriage from day one
to today? If you and your spouse made an average of 10 mistakes
a week times 52 weeks, that's 520 mistakes a year. If you've been
married 10 years, that's 5,200 mistakes. That means if you've been
married a long time—Congratulations! Over a pretty substantial
period of time you've probably worked through some tough issues
and you should be recognized for your efforts.

God calls us to love one another deeply, from the heart. For
your marriage, that means growing, working, and loving each
other, despite the mistakes you make. Remember, "love ... keeps
no record of wrongs" (1 Corinthians 13:4-5).

MARRIAGE MOMENTS

❖ In what areas have you and your spouse grown?
❖ What can help you continue this trend of growth?

PRAY TOGETHER

TWICE AS NICE

ECCLESIASTES 4:9

"Two are better than one, because they have a good return for their work."

As married couples, it seems there is typically one spouse who is dealing with a particular trial or stressful situation. Along with the help of God, the other spouse can be supportive, provide comfort, and help to weather the storm. Unfortunately, many times, after one spouse's storm has passed, the other spouse has an issue that needs to be addressed. There usually seems to be something pushing and pulling at one or the other spouse.

Here are a few action steps you can take to help you avoid drifting apart and stay connected as a couple during these times:

- Talk in an open and honest way, expressing your thoughts and feelings.
- Plan by anticipating as much as possible upcoming seasons of difficulty.
- Pray for each other and as a couple.
- Spend time together in a relaxed and fun way.

MARRIAGE MOMENTS

❖ What are some storms that you have weathered or are weathering?
❖ What can you do to navigate those difficult times more effectively?

PRAY TOGETHER

Look beyond the Current Crisis

PHILIPPIANS 4:11

"I am not saying this because I am in need, for I have learned to be content whatever the circumstances."

Many couples have experienced the pain and suffering of a spouse contracting a serious illness. This can be exhausting and emotional and can put any marriage to the test, as one spouse deals with fatigue and frailty and the other experiences the mounting burdens. It's important during this time that couples look beyond the current crisis and see the situation from God's perspective. It can be difficult, but it is critical to try to stay positive, both for your own peace of mind and for that of your spouse and family.

This doesn't mean you won't experience moments of frustration and doubt, but with God's help you can get through anything. This is true for all situations of conflict and crisis that you might face in your marriage. No matter what it is, with God you can learn to be content in all situations. That doesn't mean ignoring the tough issues, but it does mean that through the power of Christ you can find joy even when dealing with extreme trials.

MARRIAGE MOMENTS

❖ What are some things that you are grateful for today?
❖ Is there an issue in your marriage that needs to be addressed? Can you do so with a joyful heart?

PRAY TOGETHER

IGNITING THE MARRIAGE FLAMES

JAMES 2:26
*"As the body without the spirit is dead,
so faith without deeds is dead."*

The current divorce rate for Americans continues to hover around 50 percent, which is a clear indication that we stink at marriage! One of the main reasons for the poor marriage rate could be the inability to deal with change and disappointment.

Many people enter into marriage believing it will be the end-all source of happiness in their lives. They underestimate the amount of time and energy a successful marriage requires. That's why the fire in many marriages burns out. But instead of letting the embers slowly die, make a decision today to ignite your marriage. Put your whole heart into it and be the slow burning log that serves as the base of the fire.

Don't wait on your spouse to respond better, be nicer, or change a behavior. Decide today to make some changes in yourself by asking, "What can I do to improve my marriage?" Ask God to help you. Turn the focus on you and your role in an effort to ignite the flames of your marriage relationship!

MARRIAGE MOMENTS

❖ What area of your marriage has been neglected lately?
❖ What can each of you do to make your marriage better?

PRAY TOGETHER

MARRIAGE DISTRACTION

MATTHEW 6:33

*"But seek first his kingdom and his righteousness,
and all these things will be given to you as well."*

It's easy to become distracted while driving. Many drivers have unfortunately learned to multitask while behind the wheel. They've learned that it's possible for them to smoke, talk on a cell phone, shave, or apply cosmetics while driving. Dangerous? Definitely. It seems many have forgotten that when they are behind the wheel the primary purpose is to drive.

The same can be said for marriage. Often we get distracted and forget our primary focus is the relationship. That includes forgetting to invite God into this union. He's the One who created marriage. We try to juggle several balls and unintentionally take our eyes off our spouse. That's what can drive the relationship off the road.

Your jobs, kids, and friends can often distract you from your marriage, but with God's help and your focus redirected, you can get back on course.

MARRIAGE MOMENTS

❖ What are the things distracting you from the main focus of marriage?

❖ What do you as a couple and as individuals need to change to get your marriage back in focus?

PRAY TOGETHER

GIVE 'EM SOMETHING TO TALK ABOUT

COLOSSIANS 3:12
"Therefore, as God's chosen people, holy and dearly loved, clothe yourselves with compassion, kindness, humility, gentleness and patience."

Most divorces in the United States occur in the second year of marriage. Many counselors feel that this is due to the inability of newly-married couples to communicate effectively and resolve their differences. Hurts and misunderstandings are inevitable in any marriage. People who separate and divorce are those who can't forgive, reconcile, or restore closeness after these times of conflict.

Studies show that couples who receive training in how to communicate and resolve conflicts show a huge increase in marital satisfaction, communication, conflict management, and forgiveness. The Bible has a lot to say about these specific areas.

The key to any successful marriage, especially in the early years, is to learn relationship skills by talking together, reading books or watching programming on the subject, attending couples' retreats, going to counseling, and reading God's Word. These efforts will help you as you work toward achieving a healthy marriage relationship.

MARRIAGE MOMENTS

❖ In the last six months, have you as a couple gotten better or worse at communicating?

❖ What are some things you as a couple can do, or what have you done, to improve your communication?

PRAY TOGETHER

DOES MARRIAGE IMPROVE WITH AGE?

JOB 12:12

*"Is not wisdom found among the aged?
Does not long life bring understanding?"*

Your relationship with the Lord should improve the longer you work at it if your heart is in the right place. That doesn't mean it will always be perfect, but over time it should improve.

Your marriage should also get better with age. Some people who have been married for twenty years or more may feel as though they have nothing to look forward to in their marriage, because it's easy for things to stagnate—and perhaps even deteriorate—over the years.

Couples need to continually give to their marriage in order for it to be successful. If you've stopped contributing to your marriage, you need to invest time, energy, and emotion right away. Otherwise, your marriage will begin to lose its luster and not feel exciting or look attractive.

Marriages that survive for any length of time don't do so by accident. Take time to focus now on one or two things you can do to make your marriage feel exciting and new.

MARRIAGE MOMENTS

❖ What can you do to add newness to your marriage, so it improves with age?
❖ Is your marriage better now than it was six months ago, or one year ago, or five years ago?

PRAY TOGETHER

DO AS YOU SAY

EXODUS 12:24
*"Obey these instructions as a lasting ordinance for you
and your descendants."*

Sometimes we know the right way to do something to the point that we could instruct others on how to do it, but that doesn't mean we will do it that way. Think of Christians you may know who can quote Scripture easily but haven't really learned to hide God's Word in their heart. Or you may find yourself reading a book on how to improve communication in your marriage but never actually put the concepts into practice.

Many times it is easier to give than receive when it comes to advice. How many times do you have advice for your spouse on how to change, but don't look in the mirror?

To bring honor to God, our behaviors and words need to be consistent and match what we are encouraging others to say and do.

MARRIAGE MOMENTS

❖ Are there inconsistencies in your words or behaviors?
❖ What changes do you need to make today?

PRAY TOGETHER

ARE YOU COMPATIBLE?

1 CORINTHIANS 12:4
"There are different kinds of gifts, but the same Spirit."

Research has shown that the more a couple shares in common regarding their personality traits, the more harmony the marriage has in general. Some of you reading this will agree for obvious reasons. Yet others might read this and panic since the person they're married to is the exact opposite of themselves in many areas. He enjoys cooking and she does not. She is spontaneous, while he wants everything planned in advance. He's a spender and she's a saver.

No matter how you respond to this idea of compatibility in marriage, the key is getting the differences in your marriage to work for you. God created us all different for a reason. He designed marriage so that one person's gifts would complement the other person's, so that together they would build up God's kingdom. Great couples navigate their discrepancies and don't allow their differences to tear them apart. They view their individual gifts as a strength, not a weakness.

MARRIAGE MOMENTS

❖ What differences are causing the greatest strain in your relationship?
❖ What are you doing to deal with these differences so they can be a help, not a hindrance?

PRAY TOGETHER

Run from Harm

PROVERBS 18:10

*"The name of the LORD is a strong tower;
the righteous run to it and are safe."*

If there is something causing you great stress and harm in your marriage, run away from it and toward the Lord by getting on your knees in prayer! That doesn't mean you should abandon your responsibilities or refuse to work on your problems. The idea is that if your stress is due to things like being overcommitted in your volunteer work or devoting too much time to watching television or spending too much money on material items, then you need to get away from those things.

Imagine that you have a cat on your porch that isn't yours and you keep feeding it every night. Chances are pretty good that the cat is going to stay on your porch if you keep putting out the food. But if you stop feeding it and shoo it away, it will probably disappear. It's pretty simple stuff. Run away from the stuff that's creating harm and stress in your marriage and run to the Lord. Bring to Him your struggles and your successes, and watch your marriage flourish.

MARRIAGE MOMENTS

❖ What is causing harm or stress in your marriage?
❖ How can you make those things disappear?

PRAY TOGETHER

Love Can Build a Bridge

PROVERBS 10:12

"Hatred stirs up dissention, but love covers over all wrongs."

If you've ever been through a construction zone where a bridge is being built, you know you need a lot of patience. There are a lot of orange cones and barrels to maneuver around, and traffic tends to get backed up in these areas. What's best in these situations is to turn on the radio, take a deep breath, relax, and give yourself some extra time.

The same can be true when you and your spouse have a disagreement or some kind of setback in your relationship. It can seem as though every time you communicate, you have to dodge more orange cones. The wait for a time to work on the relationship can seem interminable. Love is the bridge that can connect you back together. The best example of this is Christ dying on the cross and bridging the gap between God and people.

There may be issues you need to get around or subjects that are blocking your capacity to be close. Let the love you have for each other help you to overcome these differences. Let it be the bridge that keeps you connected when you feel a gap in your marriage.

MARRIAGE MOMENTS

❖ How connected do you feel right now in your marriage?
❖ In what areas of your marriage do you need to set aside differences and love your spouse?

PRAY TOGETHER

WHAT DO YOU ENJOY?

ECCLESIASTES 4:9

*"Two are better than one, because they have a good return
for their work."*

If someone asked you and your spouse the question, "What do you enjoying doing together?" could you immediately come up with two or three activities you like to do as a couple? Now there might be one obvious answer, although the question isn't referring to sex but to something you could do publicly in front of others.

Just as spending time with the Lord is important to building your relationship with Him, it's important that you spend time together as husband and wife. Maybe it's riding bikes, hunting for antiques or watching sports and cheering on your favorite team. If you hesitated and struggled to come up with an answer, then maybe you need to spend some time thinking about something enjoyable you could do as a couple. It's important that you not just co-exist but enjoy life together.

MARRIAGE MOMENTS

❖ What could you add to the list of activities you share with each other?

❖ If you struggled for an answer, what can you do to change that?

PRAY TOGETHER

FEEDBACK

EPHESIANS 4:15

"Instead, speaking the truth in love, we will in all things grow up into him who is the Head, that is, Christ."

Evaluation and feedback function together as the cornerstone for success in sales and marketing. This combination is a tool that is used by teachers, seminar leaders, business owners, and others who provide services to clients and customers. The Bible supplies feedback for Christians in how they are supposed to live their lives. Why not use that same method for finding out how others view your marriage? If you have children, you could start with them. Ask them to comment on what they have learned thus far from observing your marriage. If you don't have children, ask trusted friends or other family members.

Be prepared to receive honest feedback, and then take what you learn and make changes that will positively affect your marriage. Finally, don't forget to celebrate the great comments you receive.

MARRIAGE MOMENTS

❖ What do you think people will say?
❖ How will you prepare yourselves for truthful feedback?

PRAY TOGETHER

GROWING IN PHYSICAL INTIMACY

SONG OF SOLOMON 2:16
"My lover is mine and I am his; he browses among the lilies."

Intimacy with God looks different for everyone. For some this may mean attending church weekly, while for others it may mean hours spent studying the Bible. For some it might mean quiet time just listening, while for others it might mean in-depth times of sustained prayer.

Intimacy will also look different for spouses with regard to their sexual and physical needs. Many researchers assert that the capacity for intimacy is learned through the touch and holding you received in your childhood. Your views and expectations of intimacy, whether positive or negative, developed from what you learned in those early years.

Intimacy is a learned behavior that can be changed if you are willing to take the necessary steps to work on it and grow in your relationship. If your intimacy needs were never developed, you will need to learn how to give and receive pleasure so that your marriage can continue to grow.

Intimacy is a great way for couples to stay connected. Be aware of each other's personal and nonsexual touch needs. This is an essential ingredient in the recipe for a great marriage.

MARRIAGE MOMENTS

❖ When was the last time you spent time as a couple talking about this area of your relationship?
❖ What are some changes you can make to help with this area of your relationship?

PRAY TOGETHER

GO THE EXTRA MILE

1 CORINTHIANS 12:25
"So that there should be no division in the body,
but that its parts should have equal concern for each other."

God created women to be more relationship oriented. It's not unusual, then, for the burden of the relationship to fall on the woman. Often, she is expected to "make it work." When the husband exerts minimal effort with regard to the relationship, it's often seen as "good enough."

This is not true in all marriages; nor should women stop doing as much as they can to make their marriage great. The challenge is for men who aren't pulling their portion of the load to lean in and give an equal amount of effort to maintaining their marriage. Men need to invest as much in their marriage and their families as they do in their jobs. This includes providing loving leadership in the areas of finances and spirituality and avoiding negative and self-absorbed attitudes. Both spouses need to strive to go the extra mile in making the marriage work.

MARRIAGE MOMENTS

❖ What are a couple of areas in particular in which your husband can grow that will help the marriage?

❖ What are some things your wife can do to encourage you positively in those areas of growth?

PRAY TOGETHER

RISKY BUSINESS

PSALM 147:5
"Great is our Lord and mighty in power;
his understanding has no limit."

Research about cohabiting couples has been conducted by several universities, such as Yale and the University of Chicago. These studies have shown many risks and liabilities associated with living together prior to marriage. They have revealed that those who live together prior to marriage have higher separation and divorce rates. Another surprising statistic was that unions begun by cohabitation are almost twice as likely to dissolve within ten years, compared to all other first marriages.

Overall, the research shows that living together without being married is risky business and may create serious relational problems down the road for the couple.

If you have been in a live-in situation prior to marriage, you may be faced with some unique challenges; however, God can work in your life and marriage in powerful ways if you seek His help. Be aware of the possible pitfalls and have a plan ready to overcome them.

MARRIAGE MOMENTS

❖ How can you as a couple create more oneness in your marriage?
❖ Are you influencing your children and others in ways that will help them make good choices for their relationships?

PRAY TOGETHER

A Little Coaching Goes a Long Way

1 THESSALONIANS 4:18

"Therefore encourage each other with these words."

If in your school years you played an organized sport, participated in gym class, had a part in a play, or participated in a spelling or geography bee, you were probably coached. This coaching was necessary for you to learn the fundamentals of the activity. If you had a good coach, they knew how to motivate you to do your best by encouraging you even when you didn't feel like performing. For instance, Michael Jordan is considered to be one of the greatest basketball players ever in the NBA, but his team didn't win any championships until it was paired with the right coach.

We have all needed coaching at one time or another as we grew up; sometimes we even need coaching as adults—say, in our jobs. We also need it in our marriages as we navigate the sometimes turbulent waters. Although God is the ultimate marriage coach, it may be helpful to find an individual or couple to mentor you and your spouse. Pick someone who is encouraging and who genuinely cares about you and your marriage.

MARRIAGE MOMENTS

❖ Who can you find who would "coach" you on your marriage?
❖ What types of issues might the person help coach you on?

PRAY TOGETHER

THE WORRY FACTOR

MATTHEW 6:34

"Therefore do not worry about tomorrow, for tomorrow will worry about itself. Each day has enough trouble of its own."

It's easy to spend a tremendous amount of time and energy investing in things that have no real value. This can include activities such as watching a lot of mindless television or any task that occupies a lot of our time but doesn't result in a gain.

Similarly, nonproductive time spent worrying has no value. This could be defined as time spent anticipating or planning for things that are either out of your control or will probably never happen. Some of this is normal and everyone is guilty of it, but consider how much of your time as individuals or as a couple is spent worrying. If you stopped and thought about it and added up the minutes, how much of your communication is wasted on the "worry factor"?

Using tally marks, try keeping track on a sheet of paper of the number of minutes that you spend worrying during a day. It may surprise you how much of your time is focused on something that is nonproductive and could be considered destructive, especially to your marriage. A pastor once asked, "Why pray when you can worry?" Think about it.

MARRIAGE MOMENTS

❖ What is your biggest area of worry (finances, children, school, work, etc.)?

❖ How can you as a couple spend more time focused on good and productive things?

PRAY TOGETHER

WHEN GOD SAYS NO

1 CORINTHIANS 2:7

"No, we speak of God's secret wisdom, a wisdom that has been hidden and that God destined for our glory before time began."

Infertility is one of the most painful problems a couple can face. The inability to conceive affects every aspect of life, often bringing about emotional upheaval, marital strain, financial stress, and many other concerns. Infertility affects about 6.1 million people in the United States. About 40 percent of infertility cases are attributed to men and 40 percent are seen as the result of female factors, with the remaining 20 percent being unexplained or a problem caused in both partners.

Couples who deal with infertility often wonder whether they are somehow being punished by God. They tend to feel isolated and frequently struggle with the problem alone. This issue, like many others, is one that needs broader support in the form of medical, relational, or spiritual help. Asking for help is the first step toward wholeness in the face of infertility.

Maybe this is something you have dealt with, or perhaps others in your family or group of friends have experienced this issue. Whatever the case, either ask for help or offer help and make it a "we" effort.

MARRIAGE MOMENTS

❖ How could you as a couple respond to your own or others' infertility in a more effective way?

❖ In general, how could you be more outwardly focused to support others on a variety of issues?

PRAY TOGETHER

WE WILL SURVIVE!

PSALM 55:22
"Cast your cares on the LORD and he will sustain you;
he will never let the righteous fall."

Why do some marriages survive while others do not? While there are many reasons why marriages fail, there is research that suggests a few possible reasons why some marriages survive.

A marriage has a good chance of surviving when partners have the ability to stubbornly outlast their problems. Even though stress issues will come and go, these couples vow to stay committed. Eventually marital satisfaction increases.

Another reason a marriage has a better chance of surviving is that a husband and wife actively work to solve problems in their relationship, as opposed to ignoring issues or denying that there are difficulties in the first place. Personal happiness is another factor that seems to contribute to successful long-term marriages. Individuals who work on their own happiness and strive to bring resolution to their personal struggles may have better success in staying married for life.

MARRIAGE MOMENTS

❖ Based on the above considerations, do you believe your marriage will survive?
❖ If you answered no, what steps can you incorporate to improve the chances of your marriage surviving?

PRAY TOGETHER

THE POWER
OF ENCOURAGEMENT

2 THESSALONIANS 2:16-17
*"May our Lord Jesus Christ encourage your hearts
and strengthen you in every good deed and word."*

Have you heard the phrase, "If you don't have anything good to say, then don't say anything at all"? It's used as a warning to encourage people to use kind words with one another. Harsh or negative comments can be so defeating and hurtful. Sometimes words that were used to attack us can stick with us for a lifetime.

As a couple, think about the amount of encouragement you have in your household. Are there five positive comments to one negative comment, or is the ratio in your marriage more like ten to one? Some couples have experienced a one-to-one ratio—or worse.

How do you and your spouse speak to one another? Be careful what you say and do because your words and actions have a huge impact on other people. Choose to say positive things and to be an encourager to those around you. Make your legacy and that of your marriage one of encouragement and kind words.

MARRIAGE MOMENTS

❖ What is the ratio of positive to negative comments in your marriage?

❖ What can each one of you do specifically to change the tone in your marriage to make it more positive?

PRAY TOGETHER

SEASONS OF MARRIAGE

ECCLESIASTES 3:1
*"There is a time for everything, and a season
for every activity under heaven."*

Every marriage passes through many seasons. There may be seasons of no children, job changes, changing addresses, seasons of the first child, seasons of several children, and then seasons of no children again. With each season encountered, there are new and different demands. Each season comes with its own unique set of challenges. With children there are challenges of sleep deprivation, time constraints, and differences in disciplining. Job changes sometimes demand many long hours and complete focus. The empty-nest syndrome may cause loneliness or boredom.

As you reflect on your marriage and the different seasons you have been or will go through, think about both the good and difficult aspects to each season. God is aware of all the seasons and can help you through each one of them.

MARRIAGE MOMENTS

❖ What has been your favorite season so far and why?
❖ What has been your most difficult season so far and why?

PRAY TOGETHER

WHERE IS YOUR TREASURE?

MATTHEW 6:21

"For where your treasure is, there your heart will be also."

God knows what is important to us because He sees where we spend our time and money. Does your spouse know where your treasure is? Are there ways that you show your spouse they are treasured by you?

To figure out where your treasure is, just look at where you spend most of your time and money. Wherever you spend your time or focus your energy, that's probably one of the top priorities in your life. When couples spend time together it will ultimately help their relationship to be better. When couples spend money on things that will help nurture their relationship, this, too, will impact their marriage in a positive way.

Make sure you are spending time and money on your marriage relationship. If you do, your heart and emotions will follow.

MARRIAGE MOMENTS

❖ Where does your spouse feel that your focus and energy are being directed?

❖ If your spouse doesn't feel treasured, what can you do to change that?

PRAY TOGETHER

Drip Stoppers

PROVERBS 5:3-4

"The lips of an adulteress drip honey, and her speech is smoother than oil; but in the end she is bitter as gall, sharp as a double-edged sword."

There are days when a spouse can be easily seduced into thinking that the candy in one jar is sweeter than that in another. They believe they can find someone better than the person they married. Many people fall into this temptation. But, most often, what appears to be sweeter than sweet quickly becomes bitter and destructive.

The wise couple has surrounded themselves with guards to protect their marriage. Take time today to establish some "drip" stoppers that will save you in the long run. Think of the consequences of divorce for everyone involved. Recognize the blessings in your life. Seek to pursue God's best for your life and your marriage, which is always His plan—staying happily married for life!

MARRIAGE MOMENTS

❖ How have you divorce-proofed your marriage?
❖ What can you do to sweeten up your relationship?

DIFFERENT IS GOOD

1 CORINTHIANS 12:20
"As it is, there are many parts, but one body."

Every spouse does marriage a little differently. That's because, individually, each of us is different and we have different needs, desires, talents, and gifts. That's what makes life and relationships so interesting! God designed the body of Christ to be made up of a multitude of people, each with different gifts, who are unified in spirit and faith. The idea is for each of us to use our gifts to promote His kingdom.

You and your spouse bring unique gifts to your marriage, but you are to come together unified in spirit. Ignore external comments or input that people might give you about your marriage if such comments offer no added value. If you are honoring God and cherishing each other, then ignore idle words and manage your marriage in a way that is pleasing to God, not to other people.

MARRIAGE MOMENTS

❖ What do you most enjoy about your marriage?
❖ What can you change to make your marriage even better?

FORBIDDEN WORD

PROVERBS 15:1
"A gentle answer turns away wrath, but a harsh word stirs up anger."

God is certainly not a fan of divorce, and couples should do whatever it takes to avoid it. Some couples get married and make a vow to not use the word *divorce* as part of their vocabulary. It is especially important that it not be used in the heat of a moment or as a manipulative tool to get someone to change a behavior. Even though it seems trivial, by refraining from using the word couples will tend to think much less about divorce as an option.

If you verbalize something over and over, there will be a tendency to start believing what you are saying. If you refer to your spouse using a derogatory name, pretty soon you may come to think of them in a different way. Keep the word *divorce* out of your marital vocabulary.

MARRIAGE MOMENTS

❖ Have you vowed to eliminate the word *divorce* from your conversations?

❖ Are there other words you have used during arguments that were less than flattering?

PRAY TOGETHER

IDENTIFY AND DIE

COLOSSIANS 3:5
*"Put to death, therefore, whatever belongs to your earthly nature:
sexual immorality, impurity, lust, evil desires and greed,
which is idolatry."*

Just as we are to identify with Christ and die to self, married couples should identify selfish behaviors and die to them. Is there something in your marriage that consumes your time and attention to the detriment of your relationship? Are you insisting on having your way on some issue? If so, take the time to understand what the repercussions of this activity are for your marriage, and consider how you might change your priorities. The idea of "dying to" this activity might be new, but consider what it might mean for you.

The world's philosophy says it's okay to indulge yourself in certain areas, But is that beneficial to your marriage? Your commitment to your spouse needs to come first. Examine your life and your practices and identify that thing that borders on selfishness. If you can't figure out what that might be, then ask your spouse to help you find it. You will both benefit in the end and win mutually at home.

MARRIAGE MOMENTS

❖ What issues came immediately to mind after reading this?
❖ Was it easier for you to identify issues for your spouse? Why?

PRAY TOGETHER

Making Values Mesh

1 JOHN 1:6
*"If we claim to have fellowship with him yet walk in the darkness,
we lie and do not live by the truth."*

Every person has his or her own unique set of values, which have been shaped over time and influenced by a variety of things, including gender, ethnicity, education, family background, religious beliefs, and significant past experiences. In marriage, however, values get tricky—especially, for example, when she values being on time for appointments and he values a loose schedule.

Just as Christians should align their values with God, so also couples have to learn how to mesh their values together. Every couple has shared values that are helpful on the road to marital bliss. These values are essential to the overall growth of the relationship. They're the seasoning that enhances and flavors the marriage. At the same time, each spouse also holds on to some values that can be harmful to their marriage. These values can surround such complex issues as relationships and religion and such simple issues as recycling or routine.

It's important that couples take time together to discuss these differences, being careful to name and describe them and their relative importance in each spouse's life. Once this is done, a couple can begin to figure out what values are beneficial and what values should be overruled.

MARRIAGE MOMENTS

❖ What values did each of you grow up with?
❖ Which values are important for you to keep and which should be tossed aside?

PRAY TOGETHER

THE FAB FOUR

SONG OF SOLOMON 1:4
"Take me away with you—let us hurry!
Let the king bring me into his chambers."

Think back to the last occasion you had time alone with your
spouse. Can you remember it? Take a look at these four different, fabulous ways to spend time together.

Connections: Build a routine of spending one-on-one time
together at least twenty to thirty minutes a day. Spend time touching base with what's going on in your lives.

Dates: Schedule dates at least weekly or bimonthly. Keep things
light by holding hands and enjoying each other's company.

Extended Dates: Every few months, schedule a longer time together, like a full day away from your usual surroundings. It can be
lavish or low-key, as long as it's saturated with in-depth sharing.

Getaways: Once or twice a year, schedule an overnight date or
a weekend/weeklong getaway so you can be alone for an extended
period of time. Wherever it is, be sure that you relax, rekindle,
and refresh your marriage.

It may take some adjusting of schedules and a little give-and-
take in other meaningful commitments, but connecting with your
spouse in all these ways is essential and invaluable.

MARRIAGE MOMENTS

❖ When was the last time you did any of the Fab Four?
❖ What can you do to incorporate the Fab Four into your life?

PRAY TOGETHER

ODE TO EMPTY NESTERS

SONG OF SOLOMON 8:6

"Place me like a seal over your heart, like a seal on your arm;
for love is as strong as death, its jealousy unyielding as the grave.
It burns like blazing fire, like a mighty flame."

When Jesus ascended into heaven, the Father seated Him at His right hand. God placed all things under His feet and appointed Him to be head over everything for the church. That's why we as Christians need to put God first in our life—before everything and everyone else, even our spouse. That means that our spouse should be second in our life and that, if we have kids, they should come after our spouse.

Are you prioritizing in that order? If you aren't, then when your kids leave the nest someday, your relationship as a couple will suffer. It will be difficult for you to fly along together after the nest is empty. That's why it's important for your kids to see you enjoy each other as a couple. If you are not sure what you like to do together, develop a "bucket list" of things you've always wanted to do—including both short-term and long-term activities and goals, and then see how many items you can cross off the list.

MARRIAGE MOMENTS

❖ What do you like to talk about when you are alone?
❖ What do you enjoy doing together as a couple?

PRAY TOGETHER

It Can Happen

GALATIANS 6:9

"Let us not become weary in doing good, for at the proper time we will reap a harvest if we do not give up."

Cherishing your spouse is not just about showing affection and buying gifts. It's about not growing weary of the journey. It's about valuing today as being better than yesterday. Then, as years pass, and you keep reaching toward new levels of trust and intimacy in your marriage, you'll discover that you've arrived at a place you never would have believed was reachable. Think about how the Lord never grows weary of us and how we can continually reach new levels of joy with Him.

It can happen in your marriage too. You can experience that same kind of joy.

When you choose to value your spouse over other things, it is the equivalent of turning your wedding vows into everyday actions. In doing so, you communicate that your marriage is bigger than the both of you, bigger than yesterday's big brawl, bigger than today's mountain of a disagreement, bigger than tomorrow's unforeseen disaster. This won't happen in one day, one week, or even in a single year. This kind of building takes time. Intentionally build positive action into your marriage every single day.

MARRIAGE MOMENTS

❖ What steps can you take to develop a more cherishing attitude toward your spouse?

❖ What don't you currently value in your marriage that perhaps you should?

PRAY TOGETHER

WATCH FOR SIGNS

PSALM 85:10

*"Love and faithfulness meet together; righteousness
and peace kiss each other."*

When your spouse is unusually quiet, shows a decreased desire to be around you, or their mood toward you is different, do you ask them about it? Often we avoid this kind of confrontation in marriage, because it takes time and effort and we don't want to hear the answer to the question "Have I done something to offend you?" We figure eventually that the mood will pass and so we ride it out.

Over time, three, four, or five of these episodes will start to build up pressure and frustration. Soon, like an overfilled water balloon, the situation will explode. Don't wait until it's too late. Talk to your spouse when this occurs. Just as we are taught to regularly communicate with God, it's essential to have regular communication in your marriage in order to deal with all aspects of life—both the good ones and the challenging ones.

MARRIAGE MOMENTS

❖ How do you make communication a priority in your marriage?
❖ How will you address issues like this in the future?

MORE TOUCH

MATTHEW 14:35-36

*"People . . . begged him to let the sick just touch the edge
of his cloak, and all who touched him were healed."*

God designed our bodies with over five million touch sensors,
most of which are in our hands. That's an indication that He
expects affection to be part of our life and certainly a big part of a
marital relationship. Research shows that meaningful touches on
a consistent basis add two years to your life span. Touching, the
kind that doesn't always lead to sex, is an essential part of your
marriage.

It's important that you are aware of how much you do or
don't touch your spouse. A hand on the small of her back. An
arm around his shoulder. A simple hug. These are all terrific ways
to relay confidence, affirmation, pride, and support. In a hectic
world, small touches are a quick and easy way to convey love to
your spouse.

MARRIAGE MOMENTS

❖ How do you feel about giving/receiving touch from your
spouse?
❖ How can you make touch a regular practice in your relationship?

PRAY TOGETHER

KNOCK DOWN WALLS

HEBREWS 3:8

*"Do not harden your hearts as you did in the rebellion,
during the time of testing in the desert."*

God never changes. He is the same today as He was yesterday, and He will be the same tomorrow as He is today. If your relationship with God is different, it's not because of Him.

A marriage relationship is also subject to change. Even the best marriage relationships run up against brick walls. It could be the result of an unresolved argument or a petty remark that you can't seem to let go. If there is a wall between you and your spouse, do your part to knock away some bricks. Don't wait for your spouse to start—go first! No doubt several bricks have been placed there from your side anyway.

Walls become rooms, rooms become buildings, buildings become towers, and towers become cities until pretty soon the distance is too great. Knock them down before that happens.

MARRIAGE MOMENTS

❖ What "walls" have been built in your relationship?
❖ What first step can you take to start tearing down the walls?

PRAY TOGETHER

Pray for Your Spouse

JAMES 5:16

"Therefore confess your sins to each other and pray for each other so that you may be healed."

Sometimes marriages need supernatural help in order to survive. That's the kind of help that can only come from God. Maybe you are concerned because you don't know how to approach your spouse on a certain set of issues. Or perhaps you're uncomfortable sharing your own needs with your spouse—either because they haven't asked, or you don't want to burden them.

God commands us to pray for one another; that command certainly includes your spouse. You can pray for your spouse's unspoken needs or take some time to ask for their specific needs. Research has shown that couples who pray together have a divorce rate of less than 1 percent.

There is nothing more intimate than praying *with* your spouse and *for* your spouse. You can even pray for your spouse when you're mad or frustrated with them. It will amaze you how that one simple act will help to ease your anger.

MARRIAGE MOMENTS

❖ In what way can you pray for your spouse?
❖ How can you ensure you get prayer requests from your spouse in the future?

Don't Make Excuses

JOHN 15:22

"If I had not come and spoken to them, they would not be guilty of sin. Now, however, they have no excuse for their sin."

When we choose to disobey God, there will always be consequences, but there won't be excuses. God commands us to confess our sins and seek forgiveness because He already knows the truth of what's been done. There's no getting around it—we need to own up to what we've done right away.

The same thing should occur in your marriage when you've disappointed your spouse. Instead of making excuses to cover yourself, own up to the facts of the situation, apologize, and get on with life. When you try to justify your actions instead of taking responsibility for them, you lose. Your excuses will only bring your spouse frustration, but your honesty will cause them to respect you.

MARRIAGE MOMENTS

❖ In what areas of your marriage are you making excuses?
❖ Is there an area in which you consistently disappoint your spouse?

PRAY TOGETHER

WORK STYLES

HEBREWS 10:24
"And let us consider how we may spur one another on toward love and good deeds."

God designed each of us with different personalities. There are no two people exactly alike, so it's no surprise then that each of you came to the marriage relationship with particular work styles. Perhaps one of you is always in a rush to get everything done quickly while the other person is more detailed and meticulous. One of you may emerge as the project leader and may like to order the other person around because the other may be more of a follower.

While that scenario may work fine for some couples, other couples may get frustrated by the differences in their spouse's work styles. It's important to recognize the strengths and weaknesses you each have in different areas and respect your spouse's approach to getting projects done even though it differs from your own. Your individual styles aren't wrong, just different, and are in line with how God gifted each of you. When you recognize the differences, you move toward greater understanding of each other, and you also learn how to give each other constructive feedback.

MARRIAGE MOMENTS

❖ As a couple, how do you approach projects?
❖ What about your spouse's work style do you appreciate?

PRAY TOGETHER

Secret Signals

JEREMIAH 10:23
*"I know, O Lord, that a man's life is not his own;
it is not for man to direct his steps."*

The wonder of having a relationship with God is that it's just between you and Him. He knows more about you than anyone else, even your spouse. When you cultivate this kind of a close relationship with God, it's easy to speak a silent word to Him or look up at Him in thanks when something happens that you alone know wouldn't have happened without Him.

That's also the beauty of a marriage relationship. There are times when you'll laugh together about something that nobody else would understand or you will cry only in front of each other. It's a part of sharing life together. When you establish a secret signal with your spouse, you show them that you are thinking about them at that moment, when nobody else will know. It could be a nod of the head, a wink of the eye, or some similar gesture that means something special just between the two of you. It's those secret understandings that make your relationship special.

MARRIAGE MOMENTS

❖ What secret signals do you currently have?
❖ What do you share together now that is special and that nobody else knows about?

PRAY TOGETHER

Don't Panic

1 CORINTHIANS 14:33
"For God is not a God of disorder but of peace."

God calls us to live in peace. This can only happen if we call upon the Lord for supernatural strength, especially during those times when we've received devastating news. That's when Christ can bring us a peace that passes all understanding.

How do you or your spouse react when unexpected negative news comes your way? Do you both tend to panic, or is it just one of you? If it's just one of you, is it possible that the other spouse is hesitant to share negative information with you for fear of your reaction? If this sounds like the two of you, recognize that this could become a stumbling block in your communication. It's important that you and your spouse share everything with each other because you are a team. If you are the one who panics, you need to work on changing that behavior, so your spouse feels free to share important information with you. Keeping the lines of communication open is a key part of a healthy marriage.

MARRIAGE MOMENTS

❖ Who in your marriage tends to panic or overreact to bad news?
❖ How can you change that behavior, or how can your spouse communicate bad news to you in a less stress-inducing manner?

PRAY TOGETHER

KILL THE ZINGERS

TITUS 1:8

"Rather he must be hospitable, one who loves what is good,
who is self-controlled, upright, holy and disciplined."

Throughout the Bible we are told to continually encourage one another and spur each other on to good works. This should also be true in marriage, but oftentimes it is not. No one is perfect, and there are days when one spouse will let the stress of their day or a buildup of frustration affect the way they treat their partner. Words fly out of their mouth before they have time to think.

Think about how long you've gone without saying something negative to your spouse. How many times have you felt so good and upbeat, only to be crushed by one negative phrase from your spouse? It takes effort some days to speak kindly to your mate. One negative comment to your spouse will offset twenty-five wonderful statements you have already made. Work at speaking only positively to your spouse. See how long you can go without saying anything harmful.

MARRIAGE MOMENTS

❖ How can you make sure you stop yourself before saying something hurtful to your spouse?

❖ What circumstances might cause you to say something negative to your spouse?

PRAY TOGETHER

BENEFIT OF THE DOUBT

PSALM 125:1
*"Those who trust in the Lord are like Mount Zion,
which cannot be shaken but endures forever."*

Trusting the Lord completely for everything is a constant struggle. Often we think we know what's best and take action based on our feelings, instead of basing our actions on our understanding of what is right from what we read in Scripture or from our relationship with God.

We do the same thing in marriage. We think we know where our spouse is headed in a conversation or we assume we know why they took a certain action, and we respond based on our feelings instead of waiting for them to explain the reason for their behavior. If we wait for them to explain, we are better able to understand from their perspective instead of our own. That's all part of being an attentive listener.

Listen to your spouse completely before giving your reply. In fact, there will be times it will be best not to speak. Be patient and try to give them the benefit of the doubt. Choose to interpret situations and actions of your spouse in a positive light.

MARRIAGE MOMENTS

❖ Ask your spouse whether you are a good listener.
❖ What other good listening habits can you adopt?

LET LOVE WIN

MATTHEW 12:18

*"Here is my servant whom I have chosen, the one I love,
in whom I delight."*

Loving the Lord is a choice. You either do or you don't. There is no in-between. How much you love Him will vary depending on what lengths you are willing to go to trust Him and depend on Him for your life.

The same is true for marriage. You choose to get married. You're either married or you're not. There is no in-between. Determine in your heart that you will always love your spouse. Make a commitment to stay married for life. You can start by committing to never use the word "divorce" in an argument. Be careful not to argue just for the sake of arguing or to see whether someone emerges a winner. Work together as a team. When it's better, let love win. When it's worse, let love win. Always choose love. Let commitment reign, not emotions.

MARRIAGE MOMENTS

❖ Is it important for you to always win an argument?
❖ What other boundaries have you set in order to ensure that love wins?

PRAY TOGETHER

I'VE GOT A SECRET

PSALM 90:8
"You have set our iniquities before you, our secret sins in the light of your presence."

It's important that as husband and wife you don't keep secrets from each other that are significant to your relationship. If a friend confides in you about something in their life that's personal, it's okay not to divulge that information to your spouse. But keeping a secret that involves the two of you, something with regard to your family or anything else that would affect your relationship, would be inappropriate. If significant issues arise that affect the two of you, that's the time for sharing.

Trying to withhold information that you know you should share will cause you personally to experience stress and will cause undue harm in your relationship. Secrets eventually come out and may create more damage than they might have if you would have discussed the information earlier. Don't keep secrets from your spouse. They have the potential to destroy a marriage.

MARRIAGE MOMENTS

❖ Why could a secret be so destructive to your marriage?
❖ What circumstances would make you want to keep a secret from your spouse?

PRAY TOGETHER

WHO IS ON YOUR SIDE?

2 TIMOTHY 4:17
"But the Lord stood at my side and gave me strength."

Remember playing the game Red Rover? After teams divide up and join hands, the object of the game is for individuals to run toward the other line and try to break through. If the runner can't break through, they have to stay on the other team's side. If they do break through, they get to return to their original side and take someone from the other team back with them. Whatever team gets the most people over to their side can claim victory.

With God we have a promise that He will always be on our side. Do you feel that your spouse is on your side in your marriage? If there is a heated discussion with extended family members and you are in opposition, does your spouse support you? When there is an argument with one of your children, does your spouse join in with solidarity? Be a champion for your spouse. As is appropriate, when there is conflict that involves your spouse's reputation, you're on your spouse's side first.

MARRIAGE MOMENTS

❖ When has your spouse failed to take your side?
❖ How can your spouse be a better champion for you?

PRAY TOGETHER

Thank You

1 TIMOTHY 4:4

*"For everything God created is good, and nothing is to be rejected
if it is received with thanksgiving."*

Are you thankful for your spouse? If so, do you tell them? It's easy to forget to give thanks for your spouse because they're always there for you. You are comfortable with each other and assume your spouse knows how you feel. After all, you chose to marry them and you feel as though that says it all.

Oftentimes, especially after years of marriage, spouses feel taken for granted and need to hear the other spouse say "thank you." They've done the laundry a thousand times. They've mowed the lawn weekly every summer. They've made the bed more times than they can count. They do it because it's part of a marriage and caring for a household. Take the time to notice these little things, these acts of consistency and kindness. A little recognition and thanks can go a long way toward building the kind of appreciation that can keep a marriage running smoothly and happily.

MARRIAGE MOMENTS

❖ When was the last time you told your spouse "Thank you"?
❖ What traits in your spouse are you thankful for?

PRAY TOGETHER

CHAIN REACTION

EPHESIANS 4:15

"Instead, speaking the truth in love, we will in all things grow up into him who is the Head, that is, Christ."

When only one spouse shares their heart, they often feel vulnerable and alone. It probably feels similar to those times when you pray to God but don't hear anything back. You may start to doubt or wonder whether He has heard you. If He never answered your prayers, eventually you would want to give up and stop communicating. The same situation could happen in your marriage if one of you chooses not to communicate.

In order for your marriage relationship to grow, you both need to share how you feel and what's in your heart. This includes hopes, fears, and feelings of inadequacy. Men generally have a more difficult time sharing their feelings. While this may be in part because of the culture we live in, it doesn't have to be that way.

Try to encourage each other to be more open. The more you know about each other the more supportive you can be. The more supportive you can be, the more your marriage will grow. The more your marriage grows, the more you will be in love with your spouse. It's a chain reaction toward a positive result.

MARRIAGE MOMENTS

❖ How can you encourage each other to open up?
❖ How much do you share with each other?

PRAY TOGETHER

SAYING I'M SORRY

LUKE 11:4

"Forgive us our sins, for we also forgive everyone who sins against us."

Jesus commands us to forgive one another. It doesn't mean you have to immediately forget what somebody did, but you should try to forgive them as soon as possible. Granting forgiveness not only brings peace, but it also brings a sense of closure to the situation.

When you and your spouse have an argument or you just aren't pleasant to each other, how often do you say to your spouse, "I'm sorry"? Even when you do tell your spouse you're sorry, is it spoken with sincerity? Sometimes, couples say "I'm sorry" out of obligation or out of the corner of their mouth in barely a whisper. Other times couples say it with their backs turned to each other.

What if when you owe your spouse an apology you ask for their forgiveness instead? The question "Will you forgive me?" carries a lot more meaning, depth, and emphasis. You are asking a question, waiting for a response, admitting that you hurt them and that you want their forgiveness. Asking for forgiveness is a little more humbling than just spewing out another "I'm sorry."

MARRIAGE MOMENTS

❖ How do you feel about asking your spouse for forgiveness?
❖ When do you think asking for forgiveness would be more effective than just saying "I'm sorry"?

PRAY TOGETHER

DON'T LEAVE HOME WITHOUT IT

JAMES 2:22
*"You see that his faith and his actions were working together,
and his faith was made complete by what he did."*

When you leave the house, do you make sure you have everything with you that you need? If you are going to work, you probably check to make sure you have your work keys, possibly a briefcase of some sort, a lunch, and maybe an item you promised to bring someone. If you're heading off on an errand, you want to be sure to have a list of what you need, an umbrella in case it rains, cash, and maybe a recyclable bag for carrying your stuff.

Before Christ left this world, He made sure He accomplished everything He set out to do and left nothing uncompleted. In fact, His final words were, "It is finished." When you left the house this morning, did you do everything you should have, including remembering to kiss your spouse? Did you even say good-bye? A greeting or good-bye kiss from your spouse is precious. Don't leave home without it.

MARRIAGE MOMENTS

❖ What kind of exchange happens when either of you leaves the house?
❖ What can you do to make sure your departure from your spouse is tender?

PRAY TOGETHER

A GOOD INVESTMENT

PSALM 34:8

*"Taste and see that the LORD is good; blessed is the man
who takes refuge in him."*

Your relationship with the Lord is an investment in your life. You will see great returns if you do your part in contributing daily to the effort. The Lord is already 100 percent invested in you. If you invest in Him, you can't go wrong.

Marriage is also a good investment and can have better than average returns. Like other investments, marriage can be risky, especially if you don't pay attention to the market, which is your home environment. If both of you fail to make contributions, you will lose ground and become vulnerable to loss. Contributions consist of time, energy, and creativity in order to make your investment grow to a level that pays great dividends. You can't invest in marriage on the wedding day and then never check it again for gains or losses.

MARRIAGE MOMENTS

❖ What contributions are you consistently making toward your marriage?
❖ What reaction do you have when your marriage starts to spiral downward?

PRAY TOGETHER

GIVE IT ALL YOU'VE GOT

2 CHRONICLES 15:7
*"But as for you, be strong and do not give up,
for your work will be rewarded."*

When you are experiencing challenges in your marriage, don't give up. Give it all you've got. Maybe your marriage has hit a rough patch or you're experiencing a lonely year. Perhaps it's not your marriage, but everything else in life is getting you down. Regardless, it all affects your relationship with your spouse. This may be a day when you feel like giving up. You think maybe the grass is greener on the other side. But it's not—it's artificial turf!

When your marriage hits a bump in the road like this, it's time to buckle down and really rev up your engines. Pray more fervently. Ask God how you can change and be a better spouse. This is not the time to give in to your feelings but to give up your concerns to the Lord.

MARRIAGE MOMENTS

❖ When have you experienced times like these in your marriage?
❖ What can you do to ensure you don't give up on your marriage but give your marriage up to God?

PRAY TOGETHER

Dealing with Job Loss

PSALM 34:19
"A righteous man may have many troubles,
but the LORD delivers him from them all."

Losing a job can be devastating, especially if that source of income is the primary one for your family. Even if it's a secondary income, when a job is unexpectedly lost, it brings about feelings of anger, rejection, and hopelessness. A person experiencing a job loss goes through a process similar to grieving a death.

As a spouse, your support is essential to the healing process. It is a good time to just listen to your spouse and not to be too quick to offer words like, "They didn't appreciate you anyhow" or "you're better off" or "everything will be fine." Let your spouse come to that conclusion in their own time through discussions with you. Your job is to encourage them and remind them what a great wife/husband they are and how much you appreciate them, since they will be feeling a loss of confidence.

Be diligent in prayer during this time and remember that God will provide for all of your needs. We have hope when we believe in Him, and because of Him we can achieve peace and joy regardless of our circumstances.

MARRIAGE MOMENTS

❖ What is important to remember during a job loss experience?
❖ If this hasn't happened, discuss how you would handle that situation if it did.

PRAY TOGETHER

THE IN-LAWS

1 TIMOTHY 3:5

*"If anyone does not know how to manage his own family,
how can he take care of God's church?"*

Even though you married only your spouse, you will need to embrace members of your spouse's extended family too. It's possible, due to personality differences, that you won't love your in-laws quite as much as you love your spouse. Even though the Bible commands that you leave your mother and father and cling to your spouse, it doesn't mean the relationship with your respective parents just disappears. That's why it's critical for you to learn to get along with your in-laws, even if they don't always make it easy.

It's important to set boundaries with them as it relates to your relationship. Even if your spouse criticizes their own parents, it's important that you don't criticize your in-laws. It's also okay to say no to your own parents, especially if saying yes would involve putting your spouse second. If you consider these guidelines in dealing with your parents and in-laws you should be able to maintain a healthy, respectful relationship with them.

MARRIAGE MOMENTS

❖ How would you describe your relationship with your in-laws?
❖ What would you change about the relationship you have with your in-laws?

PRAY TOGETHER

CAN YOU HEAR ME?

1 JOHN 5:14

*"This is the confidence we have in approaching God:
that if we ask anything according to his will, he hears us."*

When our prayers aren't answered in what we consider a reasonable amount of time, we sometimes wonder whether God can hear us or whether He is listening.

The same thing probably happens in your marriage. Are you frustrated that your spouse doesn't listen to you? Do you say something only to have to repeat it minutes or hours later? This can be a common problem in a marriage relationship. If it continues for too long, your spouse is bound to start thinking about giving up or will turn to someone else who will listen. This can be risky for your relationship.

There are several reasons why your spouse may not be listening. Consider whether you are monopolizing the conversation, preaching or lecturing instead of talking, complaining instead of asking, bringing up old issues instead of seeking to move forward, or voicing too many generalities. These are just some of the reasons your spouse might be tuning you out.

MARRIAGE MOMENTS

❖ How good a listener are you?
❖ Ask your spouse whether you regularly engage in any of the behaviors mentioned above.

PRAY TOGETHER

Married to the Wrong Person

ROMANS 15:5

*"May the God who gives endurance and encouragement give you
a spirit of unity among yourselves as you follow Christ Jesus."*

If differences are all it takes to make two spouses "wrong," then
there's not a single marriage out there that's right. In any given
marriage, differences abound. Take your pick: the husband wants
to golf, and the wife would rather shop. The husband wants to
go out, and the wife prefers to stay home. He's a spender; she's a
saver. He's an early riser; she likes to sleep in.

Eliminating marital differences is *not* the key to marriage success. When it comes down to it, much of what makes *him* and *her*
different is precisely what can make *them* better. She will teach
him to stretch outside his own tried-and-true limits. He will teach
her to move beyond what she's always known.

His strengths can complement her weaknesses, and her
strengths can make him stronger. She will sacrifice some things,
and he will sacrifice some things, and they'll both be better for it.
These realities remind us that human weakness provides an ideal
opportunity for God's power to be displayed.

MARRIAGE MOMENTS

❖ What are some of the major differences in your relationship?
❖ How can you learn to live with those differences?

PRAY TOGETHER

Hitching Up for the Haul

PSALM 85:10
*"Love and faithfulness meet together; righteousness
and peace kiss each other."*

A farmer owned a couple of horses that were used for carrying heavy loads. Individually each horse could pull about 4,500 pounds, but when hitched up together they were able to pull 12,000 pounds!

When you hitched up with your spouse, you also gained a partner with whom you could share the load: challenges, heartaches, joys, chores, parenting, and finances, to name a few. The combined weight of all these factors feels more manageable because you're pulling together. If you think about doing a lot of those tasks or carrying all the emotional baggage alone, it would feel lopsided and uneven without your spouse to help balance things out. Add God into the mix and nothing is impossible!

On our own, each of us can manage. But together, we can manage enough to surprise ourselves; somehow, the load lightens when we're pulling with somebody else.

MARRIAGE MOMENTS

❖ How are you working together to carry the load?
❖ Where could you step up and be more supportive?

DIE TO SELF

ROMANS 14:8

"If we live, we live to the Lord; and if we die, we die to the Lord. So, whether we live or die, we belong to the Lord."

The opposite of the essence of God is "self." That's why Satan works hard to get you focused on your own agenda and your own desires, leaving God and your spouse "out in the cold." This can easily happen if you and your spouse are focused on your own projects around the house, your jobs, or your own recreational activities or interests. You may soon discover there's no time left for each other, and in the worst-case scenario, that you actually have very little in common after years of marriage.

Don't let this happen to your marriage! Pray for wisdom from God to recognize selfishness and obediently seek to cleanse it from your life. Think of areas in your relationship that might need attention in order for you to stay committed to each other.

MARRIAGE MOMENTS

❖ What can each of you do to "die to self"?
❖ When have you experienced selfishness in your relationship?

PRAY TOGETHER

TALLY YOUR VICTORIES

PSALM 60:12

"With God we will gain the victory, and he will trample down our enemies."

God often uses challenges in our life to help build up our character, as well as to help us recognize our dependence on Him. That's part of the reason our battles are significant to us.

Marriages that last a lifetime will occasionally come up against challenges. Usually, the problems are of little significance, but your response is memorable. In light of the number of years you are together with your spouse, the number of battles could be considerable, and some of these responses may be difficult to forget. In this instance, rather than focusing on the battles, learn to count the victories. Don't be defeated by your conflicts, but rather look at them as opportunities for growth in your relationship. Celebrate each one. Working your way through each conflict will make you stronger for the battles ahead.

MARRIAGE MOMENTS

❖ How do you handle conflicts that arise in your marriage?

❖ Ask your spouse whether there is anything you can do differently in handling conflict.

PRAY TOGETHER

IT'S THE LITTLE THINGS

JAMES 1:17

"Every good and perfect gift is from above, coming down from the Father of the heavenly lights, who does not change like shifting shadows."

It's not unusual for Christians to desire to do something big for God's kingdom. But before God will give us that kind of responsibility, He wants to see our obedience in the little things. Did we shovel snow for our neighbor, invite a friend to church, or write someone an encouraging note as He asked us to do?

It's typically not the big presents on our birthday or anniversary that endear us to our spouse. It's usually the thoughtful little gestures that take place throughout the year. It's the time you brought her a cup of coffee when she was getting ready for the day or when you made him his favorite meal and it wasn't a special occasion.

The next time either of you hears the other one mention something small that your spouse would enjoy, commit it to memory and make sure you follow up on it sometime when it will be least expected.

MARRIAGE MOMENTS

❖ What little thing that your spouse did recently was a welcome surprise?
❖ What thoughtful gestures do you really appreciate from your spouse?

PRAY TOGETHER

LOVE BIG

ROMANS 8:37

*"No, in all these things, we are more than conquerors
through him who loved us."*

Love is really bigger than all of us because God is love and God is bigger than anything or anyone else. The sacrifice of His one and only Son overcame death itself. Love can't be contained, and it can conquer mountains when it's let loose. Yet our love for our spouse can be stopped in its tracks by the concerns of life. It is easy to sweat the small stuff. The dryer doesn't work. The car is making a funny noise. The dog just brought in piles of dirt from the backyard across your newly-cleaned carpets in the living room. These little irritations can raise your blood pressure and bring you down along with your marriage.

Small stuff will always infiltrate your life and your marriage. Learn to live with the minor frustrations so you can live with the peace and joy that only God can offer. Your love is big enough to overcome the small bumps in the road of your marriage.

MARRIAGE MOMENTS

❖ What happens in your relationship when life throws you a curve?
❖ How can you let love help you overcome the small stuff?

Other marriage resources from Winning At Home . . .